W9-CPB-442

DEFILED
overcoming satan's assault

By Dr. James D. Marocco

BARTIMAEUS PUBLISHING

Defiled - Overcoming Satan's Assault
Copyright © 2006
Dr. James D. Marocco

Cover design by Carrie Low

All Scriptures are from the New International Version of the Bible unless otherwise specified.

All rights reserved. No part of this publication may be reproduced, stored in a retrieval system, or transmitted in any form or by any means - electronic, mechanical, photocopying, recording, or otherwise - without the prior written permission of the publisher and copyright owners.

Published by Bartimaeus Publishing
777 Mokulele Highway
Kahului, HI 96732

ISBN 1-881227-05-7

Dedication

Dedicated to my wife, Pastor Colleen Marocco. Her love, openess, sensitivity, insight and spirituality have been a protection for me in my battle against defilement. She was also my biggest supporter in writing this book.

Acknowledgements

A special thanks to Sue Nakama, Becky Moody and Pastor Colleen Marocco who helped in the typing and editing of this book..

Special thanks also to Carrie Low who created the provocative cover.

Most of all I praise our Lord Jesus for His continued work of cleansing and giving me whatever insight the reader receives from this book that encourages and strengthens them in their Christian walk.

Table of Contents

Forward by Cindy Jacobs

I am glad you have chosen to read this book. It is life changing! The subject of defilement is rarely taught in the body of Christ, yet it is a biblical principle that is much needed.

God has given James Marocco the mandate to teach this message to His people. I am convinced that you will find wisdom that you have searched for to change your family, church, and nation contained in these pages. Once you read you will think to yourself, "Why haven't I known this before?"

Many individuals are in great bondage because their mind and consciences have been defiled. (Titus 1:15) This creates bondages that hold them captive. Through prayer, it is possible, to see the darkness penetrated.

Family systems can be defiled as well. The power of God is well able to break and penetrate every stronghold that holds those you love captive.

As you study each chapter you will come to understand that our churches, businesses, and schools need cleansing from defilement.

Dr. James Marocco is a leader who has successfully taught this subject across the face of the world. I know both he and his family on a deep personal level. He is successful not only as a senior pastor of a large and prosperous church in Maui, Hawaii; but as a parent.

Open up the pages of this book and apply the keys found in its contents. Prepare to be transformed and receive revelation knowledge that will set you, your loved ones, and the world free.

Introduction

I had just finished speaking at one of the great churches in America. It was the first service in a ministry tour that would have me for a brief time away from my ministry on Maui. It was quite late by the time I got to my hotel room after having dinner with the pastor. Since I had spent a lot of time traveling to that city, I thought I would get caught up on the day's news and turned on the television while getting ready for bed. Little did I know the battle that I had just stepped into. As I began to scan the channels in my search for the news, the first channel I turned to had strong sexual images on it. I quickly changed the station and went on to settle in on the news channel. I began to be bothered by the thought that I had pushed the wrong button on the remote and by mistake had allowed some porn service in my room. Did I really see what I perceived as I flipped through the channels? So I began to redo my steps and sure enough the sexual images were real; porn was on my room's television. I quickly shut off the television and called the front desk to inquire why such a thing was allowed in my room. The person that answered said there must be a mistake and he would fix it. He asked if I would turn the television back on in a few minutes to check again. When I did, to my shock, it was still there. At this point I realized I needed to go down to the front desk and confront the manager over this issue. He agreed to come up to my room and see if what I was saying was true. Sure enough, the porn was still there. He said he did not know why this was the case, but he went on to say something quite profound: "You are the only one who has complained." I quite forcefully expressed how allowing such a thing to take place in his hotel was wrong and the problem must be fixed. Apparently unable to do anything about the problem he left and I, alone in the room, was engulfed in a battle in my mind. On the one hand, my fallen human nature desired to express itself through lust. Demon spirits were lying to me, "Nobody will know if you watch. After all, it's not your fault that it is on your television. Besides, it won't hurt you and everyone else is watching." On the other hand, my spirit clearly reminded me of the guilt and shame that would follow if I watched; how my ministry would be compromised and how the enemy would use this to bind me. I stood in my room and prayed. The Holy Spirit spoke, "Remove this idol from your eyes." It was a clear word from *Psalm 101:3* which states, "*I will set before my eyes no vile thing.*" I immediately obeyed. I moved the huge cabinet, disconnected all the wires & cables, picked up the large TV, and deposited it in the hallway outside my room. I called the front desk to inform them of my protest against the porn in the hotel and that they could pick up their TV at any time, for it was laying in the hall. I went to sleep and the next morning a repairman showed up and asked me what was wrong with the TV. I told him, "It shows porn." When I checked out I wrote a formal complaint to the general manager of my being offended by what had happened. On my way to the airport I received a call on my cell phone from the manager apologizing and assuring me that the problem would be corrected. I could not help thinking of something my friend Jesse Duplantis shared with my congregation that the best way to handle temptation was to embarrass it.

You might be asking, "Why did you go through so much trouble and make such a big deal over watching porn, especially since it is common place today and so easily accessible?" The answer to this question deals with my understanding of the strategy of the devil to destroy the effectiveness of the body of Christ in the world today. His strategy can be summarized by one word: DEFILEMENT. Understanding defilement and how we can overcome and be victorious over it is what this book is all about.

We have all held a small child who could not hold its milk down. However, none of us would tolerate someone just vomiting on us for their pleasure and for the purpose of demeaning us. Our innate God-given desire for dignity would exhibit itself and we would protest. But imagine with me a huge crowd of people who have all been vomited on. Some are even looking for people to vomit on them more. The stench is so severe that it overwhelms us as observers even though we are standing at a distance away from the crowd. On closer examination, because the vomit has not been washed off, it has attracted all sorts of insects and parasites. Infections start breaking out over the bodies. Some have become so diseased they can no longer move, but crumple in a heap waiting to die.

What madness is this? This is a picture of what is happening in the spiritual realm. Satan has released a fountain of filth that is being vomited on a naive and foolish population. I call this defilement. If not dealt with, it leads to demonization, and from this, death. This book is an exposé of the phenomena of defilement.

I

Watch Out For the Leaven

I Corinthians 5:6-13

"Your boasting is not good. Don't you know that a little yeast works through the whole batch of dough? Get rid of the old yeast that you may be a new batch without yeast – as you really are. For Christ, our Passover lamb, has been sacrificed. Therefore let us keep the Festival, not with the old yeast, the yeast of malice and wickedness, but with bread without yeast, the bread of sincerity and truth. I have written you in my letter not to associate with sexually immoral people – not at all

meaning the people of this world who are immoral, or the greedy and swindlers, or idolaters. In that case you would have to leave this world. But now I am writing you that you must not associate with anyone who calls himself a brother but is sexually immoral or greedy, an idolater or a slanderer, a drunkard or a swindler. With such a man do not even eat. What business is it of mine to judge those outside the church? Are you not to judge those inside? God will judge those outside. 'Expel the wicked man from among you.'"

The context of this passage is fascinating. The Apostle Paul is confronting a problem in the Corinthian Church. A man is having an affair with his father's wife, his step-mother. Everyone knows about it, but no one has done anything. In fact, the church may have been haughty in their toleration of this man. The Apostle Paul states, *"Shouldn't you rather have been filled with grief and put out of your fellowship the man who did this?"* (I Corinthians 5:2) Paul goes on to command the church to *"hand this man over to Satan, so that the sinful nature may be destroyed and his spirit saved on the day of the Lord."* (I Corinthians 5:5)

What does the Apostle Paul mean by *"handing over to Satan"*? It is mentioned here in *I Corinthians 5:5* and in *I Timothy 1:20* which states, *"Among them are Hymenaeus and Alexander, whom I have handed over to Satan to be taught not to blaspheme."* It is not clear how this operates. I can only suggest what I understand and have practiced. In *Matthew 18:15-17*, it mentions that the process of discipline is personal. If someone sins, one who knows about it goes to the person privately and confronts them. If there is not repentance, then he goes back with one or two others and if there is no repentance, he takes it to the church. If he doesn't listen to the church he must be separated from the fellowship of believers.

In my case, a number of things happened early in my ministry on Maui that set me on a course of attempting to be faithful in the realm of church discipline. However, the first awareness of my role in this area began when I was pastoring in Wilmington, California working among youth. I remember a number of young people, who although raised in a Christian home, chose to reject the Gospel by their life-style choices. As their pastor I had to personally confront them over their sin.

I had to warn one young man who would repeatedly backslide about being turned over to Satan for the destruction of his flesh so his soul would be saved. Tragically, he continued in his rebellious state and ended up dying in a drug deal gone bad. But, with his family praying and the many hours that other pastors and I personally ministered to him, I can hope that in those final moments before death took him, he repented and received Christ. I grieved over the loss of a life that God could have used for His glory and the pain his family went through. However, I was thankful that I obeyed the Word to help him and was not afraid to confront him and warn him.

I continued to try to encourage people to live right when I moved to Honolulu. There I had to personally deal with a couple who got saved in our church and were living together, but were not married. I approached them about getting married, which they wanted to do but could not. Their dilemma was that one of them was married to someone else. To untangle the web of messed up relationships took some time, so my wife and I opened our home to the young lady while the legal issues were all worked out. It was very hard for them to be separated since they already saw themselves as husband and wife, but because of their desire to obey the Lord they separated until they could be legally married. This reaffirmed my awareness of the need for a pastor to be personally involved in the process of helping people live right.

However, I did not realize how important it was to God for us to follow *Matthew 18:15-17 and I Corinthians 5* until I came to Maui to pastor a small congregation of one hundred people. God gave us growth very quickly and people of all kinds were getting saved and added to the church. It was in this context that I had a dream of a couple who began to attend the church. In this dream the Lord revealed to me that they were living together, but were not married. In the dream I told God I did not want to be involved and I will never forget what I felt God say to me: "If you don't fix this problem, son, I'll fix you." I woke up in the morning fearful that if I did not deal with the problem that I would be under the chastisement of the Lord. So, I confronted them with this knowledge. They were shocked that I knew of their situation. I gave them an ultimatum; either break up or get married. They decided to end the relationship, but two weeks later they got married. This incident was a preparation by God for what I would face a few weeks later. During a conversation with one of the most influential board members of the church my wife had a word of knowledge that he was having an adulterous affair. I could not believe it, but by personally confronting him I was shocked to find out that it was true. Later that evening, praying that God would give me wisdom in this situation, I remembered *Matthew 18:15-17* and *I Corinthians 5*. I then decided that even if this cost me the church, I would obey. I returned to the offender's home with another brother and again confronted him over what he had done. He responded by demanding I leave his house. Finally, I brought it to the board of directors. I did not know how to turn someone over to Satan, but I figured that it meant that the protective hand of God's grace was lifted off of him. Satan would then be allowed to beat on him until he realized his need to repent. So we prayed, asking God to do just that. He was told that if he did not repent, he would not be able to continue coming to the church. I wrote a letter giving specific instructions of what he had to do in order to return into fellowship. The results were immediate. Within two months he was given a report from his doctor that he had a terminal illness, with a short time to live. He repented and then recovered from the illness. He also remarried his estranged wife. [1]

Why did God make my fixing a moral problem such a big deal? The Apostle Paul explains to the Corinthian church as to why they should do something about the sin of this man in the church. *"Don't you know that a little yeast works through the whole batch of dough?" (I Corinthians 5:6)* He uses the picture of the effects of yeast on dough to make the point that if the sin of this man was not dealt with it would affect the whole congregation, with others doing the same thing. What the Apostle Paul is talking about is the biblical concept of defilement.

---

1   I wish I could say everything turned out fine, but the man ended up working overseas and repeated the same sin. However, God took care of his now divorced wife. He gave her a good job and brought a loving Christian man into her life. They have been a faithful part of the church for many years.

2

What the Bible Says About Defilement

The first step in understanding defilement is to look at it from a biblical perspective in both the Old Testament and the New Testament.

In the Old Testament we are confronted by God who desires to dwell with His people. This dwelling or presence of God among His people was the basis for the covenant God made with Israel. He was to be their God, dwell with them and they would be His people, reflecting Him in the world. So real was this concept of God's presence that Moses, in pleading on behalf of the Israelites who had broken the covenant by worshipping the golden calf, said, *"If your Presence does not go with us, do not send us up from here."* (*Exodus 33:15*) Moses clearly knew the dilemma of being attached to a holy God. If God who is holy is going to dwell with His people, they too must be holy. That is why over and over again God's call to His people was, *"Be holy, because I am holy."* (*Leviticus 11:44-45, 19:2, 20:26*) The problem was that they were not holy. Therefore, God attempted to give them what I call a "holy consciousness" through the sacrificial system; the law and the priesthood.

For example, it was the job of the priests to *"distinguish between the holy and the common, between the unclean and clean"*. (*Leviticus 10:10*) This is where defilement or uncleanness comes into the picture. In his excellent commentary of Leviticus, Gordon J. Wenham gives the insight that in the Old Testament's understanding of reality, cleanness was what was normal. Defilement or uncleanness was abnormal and contagious. When tests were done for skin disease in *Leviticus 13*, if the person did not have the disease, the concluding remark was, "He is clean." Certain animals were seen as unclean because they did not conform to what was seen as normal in the animal world. "Fishes with scales and fins are clean but those without these normal aids to propulsion are unclean."[2] *(Leviticus 11:9-11)*

Certain animals were permanently unclean and so were people with a particular disease. There was also a temporary uncleanness which came about through contact with corpses, childbirth, diseases, discharge *(Leviticus 11-18)* and various sins.

The remedy to be clean once one was defiled varied between a washing, a lapse of time, or an elaborate ceremony. To not become clean when one became defiled was to come under the judgment of God. If one was permanently unclean through a skin disease, one was put outside the camp, as the Bible says, "to be cut off." One's defilement caused them to be expelled from the community of Israel. The reason for this was that the "unclean and holy must not meet."[3] It was an attempt to reinforce this "holy consciousness" among the people.

In the New Testament, the concept of defilement describes a deeper reality; a spiritual reality. In fact, the Old Testament is a picture book to the spiritual reality of the

---

2   Gordon J. Wenham, The Book of Leviticus. (Grand Rapids, MI: William B. Eerdman Publishing Company, 1979) 21.

3   Wenham 21.

New Testament. This is because God has literally come into our world through the person of His Son, Jesus the Christ. In Jesus' sacrificial death on the cross and in His resurrection, sin could now be forgiven and all who put their trust in Him could be holy. Food laws that separated Israel from fellowship with other nations and were a means of declaring that Israel was separated or holy to God were no longer needed. All could become holy through Christ for Jesus died for the whole world. God, through his Holy Spirit, has come to dwell in each human life, giving them the inner power to be conformed to Christ's image and to outwardly live holy. Christians were called saints or holy ones. That is, they have been "called by God to be His people just as ancient Israel had been (*Colossians 1:2; I Peter 1:2, 2:9-10; Exodus 19:5-6*). But this state of holiness must find expression in holy living (*Colossians 1:22; I Peter 1:15*)"⁴

Therefore, in the New Testament defilement is not physical in nature, but spiritual. It is anything that prevents us from living holy. A key text is *Matthew 15:11-20*. In this passage, Jesus redefines defilement. He states in verses 19-20, *"For out of the heart come evil thoughts, murder, adultery, sexual immorality, theft, false testimony, slander. These are what make a man 'unclean'; but eating with unwashed hands does not make him 'unclean.'"* Defilement can be the

---

4   Wenham 25.

condition of one's heart. What comes out of a person not only renders the person unclean or defiled, but also those who are affected by him. This is the message of *Hebrews 12:15*. *"See to it that no one misses the grace of God and that no bitter root grows up to cause trouble and defile many."* Here we see that unrepentant sin or unhealed hurts not only can become a *"bitter root"* that produces trouble in the person's life, but they also become a channel of defilement which affects those around them.

In *John 13* Jesus was going to wash Peter's feet. Peter protested so Jesus said in *verse 8*, *"Unless I wash you, you have no part with me."* Peter, always passionate says, *"Then Lord, not just my feet but my hands and my head as well."* But it is here in *verse 10* we read something fascinating. *"Jesus answered, 'A person who has had a bath needs only to wash his feet; his whole body is clean. And you are clean, though not every one of you."* The following verse gives us insight into Jesus' definition of clean and unclean. *"For he knew who was going to betray him, and that was why he said not every one was clean."* (*verse 11*) Judas was defiled, unclean, and when he partook of the sacrificial meal, Satan came into him. It is not by accident that Satan entered him at that time. In his commentary on Leviticus, Gordon J. Wenham states, "The most severe punishment is allotted to those who are unclean, yet presume to eat of the sacrificial offering. He will be cut off from his people."[5] The Apostle Paul took this Old Testament understanding of things and applied it to the Lord's Supper in *I Corinthians 11*. The Apostle Paul understood that God's judgment was upon the person who ate *"in an unworthy manner,"* the result being sickness or premature death. The remedy was to examine themselves and repent. Judas was defiled, unclean, as Jesus said in *John 13*, and yet he ate the Passover meal, thus experiencing the judgment of God; a giving up to Satan.

I am convinced that demonization begins with defilement. Defilement opens the door to demonization. *James 1:14-15* states, *"But each one is tempted when, by his own evil desire, he is dragged away and enticed. Then, after desire has conceived, it gives birth to sin; and sin, when it is full-grown, gives birth to death."* Defilement caters to our fallen human nature, resurrecting a passion for sin that because we belong to Christ should have been dead. But once our fallen human nature is resurrected, demons have greater access to us. It is clear that our fallen nature reflects the demonic, as Paul describes in *Galatians 5:19-21*, *"The acts of the sinful nature are obvious: sexual immorality, impurity and debauchery; idolatry and witchcraft; hatred, discord, jealousy, fits of rage, selfish ambition, dissensions, factions and envy;*

---

5   Wenham 125.

drunkenness, orgies, and the like. I warn you, as I did before, that those who live like this will not inherit the kingdom of God."

An area of our fallen human nature activated by being defiled can become a doorway to the demonic. Therefore defilement is a precursor to demonization. My book, <u>Closing the Forbidden Door</u>, brings insight into this area.

The greatest danger with defilement is not just the fact it is a precursor to demonization, but that it hinders the most essential part of our spiritual life. In *I Peter 4:7*, it states, *"The end of all things is near. Therefore be clear minded and self controlled so that you can pray."* Defilement works in the mind and takes away our "clear mindedness and self control." This affects our communion with God in prayer. Being effective in prayer with God hearing us and us hearing Him is the key to everything in life. The Apostle Peter is so concerned about this that in *I Peter 3:7*, he encourages husbands to treat their wives with respect and be considerate so that nothing will hinder their prayers. The problem is that most Christians in the West do not pray very much anyway and have no idea how important their prayers are. Therefore they tend not to be as sensitive to defilement as they should. But, if we truly understand the power of prayer and how defilement hinders it, we would yearn to live free of defilement.

So we see in the New Testament that defilement is a real phenomenon, making us vulnerable to greater bondage by the devil and hinders our prayer effectiveness. Jesus, concerned about His disciples and their being kept holy, warned them of the leaven of the Pharisees. This is the same term the Apostle Paul uses in *I Corinthians 5.* Jesus is warning them about being affected by the defilement of the Pharisees, just as the Apostle Paul was saying to be careful of the defilement that was happening in the Corinthian Church through their tolerating the sin of one of its members. Ironically, the preventing of defilement was behind the regulations that the Pharisees adhered to. In essence, the Pharisees attempted to build a protective fence around the law so they would not get close to breaking it and becoming defiled, or unclean. This fence was their "tradition" - the interpretation of the law by past rabbis and scholars. In the natural, one would think this desire to live holy would be commended by Jesus, especially since the Pharisees believed in the resurrection of the dead and that the whole Old Testament was the Word of God. Yet they came under the condemnation of Jesus because they made two basic mistakes.

The first is that they took their focus off of God and put it on themselves, thus becoming victims of religious pride. The worst kind of pride is religious pride. One thinks they are holy because they compare themselves with others, but they do not realize their focus has shifted from God to self. One becomes more concerned about what others think instead of what God thinks. God's intentions for His law which is "shalom," that is peace, wholeness, and holiness, is not seen. That is why, in His rebuke of the religious elite of his day, Jesus said in *Matthew 23:23*, *"You give a tenth of your spices—mint, dill and cummin."* That is, you tithe even on your spices. Jesus tells them they should do this. However, they were ignoring the law in regard to justice, mercy, and faithfulness.[6] They had numerous regulations concerning the Sabbath so they would not break the Sabbath day law, but they were so focused on religion that they overlooked God's desire that the Sabbath was to be a blessing to man, not a curse. Jesus said in Mark 2:27 that the *"Sabbath was made for man, not man for the Sabbath."* This problem of religious pride was also seen in the issue of fasting. They fasted, yes, but they made sure everyone knew they were fasting. They got their praise from man, but lost their reward from God.

The second mistake they made was that they failed to understand that defilement was spiritual. It was an issue of one's heart; the essence of one's relationship with God. They

6   *Luke 11:42 states, "Woe to you Pharisees, because you give God a tenth of your mint, rue and all other kinds of garden herbs, but you neglect justice and the love of God. You should have practiced the latter without leaving the former undone."*

had become so blinded spiritually that they could not see God's desire, so they criticized Jesus when He ministered to the sinner. They called Jesus a demon when He healed the sick and cast out demons. They were far from God's kingdom. In our desire to keep clean we must never lose sight of God's love and grace. The Apostle Paul gives us a warning because we are all vulnerable to defilement and therefore we must stay humble. He states in *Galatians 6:1*, *"Brothers, if someone is caught in a sin, you who are spiritual should restore him gently. But watch yourself, or you also may be tempted."* James encourages us to be sensitive to others in need and sums up the Christian life in *James 1:27* as taking care of *"orphans and widows and keeping oneself from being polluted by the world."*

So how do we live undefiled? The Apostle Paul said, *"We are not ignorant of his (Satan's) devices." (II Corinthians 2:11 - KJV)* But much of the church is ignorant and *"are destroyed from lack of knowledge." (Hosea 4:6)* Therefore, we must have an understanding of how demonic power operates to defile us. Keep in mind all demonic spirits are called in scripture *"unclean"* spirits. So any demonic activity affecting your life is a defiling spirit that is attempting to render the believer unclean. In *Zechariah 13:2*, the prophet Zechariah mentions, *"the spirit of impurity."* Could it be that unleashed upon our world is the *"spirit of impurity"* in an attempt to hinder the church's effectiveness in this last day move of God? I believe this is the case and this *"spirit of impurity"* or defilement works in three basic areas to defile us. The first is in the area of relationships.

3

Who Are You "Hanging Out" With?

The first way Satan attempts to defile us is through relationships. This is clearly seen in our opening text of *I Corinthians 5:9, "I have written you in my letter not to associate with sexually immoral people."* He goes on to define what he means in verse 11, *"But now I am writing you that you must not associate with anyone who calls himself a brother but is sexually immoral or greedy, an idolater or a slanderer, a drunkard or a swindler. With such a man do not even eat."* It is clear – defilement can flow through relationships. The

Apostle Paul makes the point that it is impossible not to interact with defiled people. *I Corinthians 5:10* states that he does not mean the people of the world or we would have to leave this world, but he means those who call themselves Christians, but are deceived, thinking it is okay to live like the world. However, it does not mean we can just go ahead and associate with anyone we want to who is not a Christian, because the warning in *I Corinthians 15:33*, still stands: *"Do not be misled: Bad company corrupts good character."* Our association with non-believers must be like that of Jesus. He came to *"seek and to save the lost."* He ate with publicans and sinners because He loved them and reached out to bring salvation to them.

The reason the Apostle Paul commands the Corinthians not to associate with immoral Christians is because he saw the church as a family that should treat each other as brothers and sisters. The problem is that this kind of closeness can become a vehicle for defilement to spread easily and rapidly. He reaffirms this when he specifically commands the church in Thessalonica to *"Keep away from every brother who is idle and does not live according to the teaching you received from us."* *(II Thessalonians 3:6)* Also in his letter to Titus he states, *"warn a divisive person once, and then warn him a second time, after that have nothing to do with him."* *(Titus 3:10)* Division is a defilement that can spread like a cancer if not dealt with at the source.

How does one's relationship with others bring about defilement? From my perspective, I see four mechanisms. The first is attitude. One's attitude and point of view changes according to who one "hangs out" with. I know this first hand. In 1967, as a young college student in California, I was on fire for the Lord. On weekends, either Friday or Saturday night, I played on my college football team, but which ever night I did not play I would go witnessing in Huntington Beach. I would join with a group of other Christians at an outreach coffee house. The group was a family who had taken over the coffee house ministry from Teen Challenge that I had previously worked with. The family was so radical that they would wear sandwich signs that read, "Repent or Burn," and preach to people standing in line at a movie theater. I was impressed with their memorizing of scripture, their constant emphasis on doing the will of God and their fervor for the Lord. In the second year of my involvement with them, they tried to pressure me to leave college and join their group, since they felt that formal education was not of God. They also became extremely critical of the organized church. I did not realize how I was being influenced by my relationship with them until I took a trip across country with my mom and brother to visit my family in Texas. I spewed out to my mom, who had been a missionary for 25 years, all the junk that I ingested from this group. One incident I will never forget was while in the car driving by a church. I saw a man entering it and I declared, "Look at that man. He is such a hypocrite!" I did not even know the man or the church, but such was the affect of my association with this group. My mom must have prayed diligently for me because instead of leaving college and joining the group, little by little I began to distance myself from them. The break finally came when I was reading *James 3:13-18*. In this text James makes a distinction between "wisdom that comes from heaven" and that which is *"earthly, unspiritual, of the devil."* As I compared the group with these criteria, it was very clear; their wisdom was not from God. What was hard for me to believe however was *verse 16* which said, *"There you find disorder and every evil practice."* How could a group who had memorized so much scripture and were concerned with doing the will of God, and who were so radical in their witness ever end up in that state? But that is exactly what happened. Within a few years the group came to believe that California was going to fall into the ocean so they moved to Arizona and then Texas. They changed their name from Teens for Christ to the Children of God. The family I had associated with was the Berg Family. Their story is one of shocking immorality and abuse. If it wasn't for God's mercy I could have become a leader in one of the vilest cults of the 20th century which ended up advocating prostitution and other sexual activities, all in the name of God. Truly every evil practice did emerge. My association with the group caused me to ingest their attitude and my separation from them began the process of freedom.

Not only is one's attitude affected by association which can become the mechanism by which defilement spreads, but also by the phenomona of transference and counter-transference. This is what counselors are warned about. One example is when a distraught wife, finding solace from a male counselor, finds herself transferring the normal affection she would have for her husband onto the counselor. Counter-transference is when the counselor, in the course of his becoming caught up with the emotions of the counselee, begins to reciprocate and transfers the normal affection he has for his wife onto the counselee. This whole situation can end up defiling not only the counselor and his client, but their respective families. This does not only happen in formal counseling sessions. It can happen at the workplace: a distraught wife talking to a sympathetic male co-worker; or a sensitive caring secretary catering to her boss who, because of work, is disengaged from time with his wife.

A third way that can bring defilement through relationships is what I call "projection." Projection is used in psychological circles to describe someone who mistakenly assumes another is doing something or feeling a particular way because they themselves have done the deed or feel that way. I use it in this sense in an example in Chapter 7. Here however, I am defining it as a demonic dynamic in which demons use a person as a conduit to project their thinking on another.

The lead singer of a famous rock group was interviewed. He was bragging about how many women he had sexual intercourse with. He described how during a concert he would mentally pick out a woman he thought was attractive and at the end of the concert, she would be back stage, ready to be a groupie. What the rock singer didn't know is that he and the person he picked out were victims of the master manipulator, Satan, and his demons. Satan had bound them and was attempting to keep them in deeper darkness through the use of projection.

How I came to an awareness of "projection" as I define it, took place in 1981, soon after I became the pastor on Maui. A guest healing evangelist, Roxanne Brandt, described in a message an incident that happened to her. She was speaking in a large church in the U.S. While sitting on the platform her mind was flooded with horrible sexual thoughts. She was shocked and immediately questioned her own holiness and began to pray. The Holy Spirit spoke to her and said, "Those are not your thoughts; they are coming from the pastor." This pastor was sitting on the platform with her. When she got up to speak, she prayed out loud, binding off demonic influence from herself and the congregation. Although she said nothing about the pastor, he immediately left the sanctuary. She soon found out the pastor was bound by pornography and at the time was having an adulterous affair. The story ended tragically with the pastor divorcing his wife, resigning his church and ultimately committing suicide. As Roxanne told the story it dawned on me that "projection" is a real phenomenon and can be the means by which the defilement is passed on. In ancient times it was referred to as a "spell" or "evil eye." A person can become a carrier of evil thoughts that infect others in much the same way that a person carrying a virus infects by their association. A tragic story that has been repeated often on Maui is when a wife or husband is at work and begins to associate with a fellow worker of the opposite sex. Not only can transference and counter-transference take place, but "projection" also becomes a real threat. Lust-filled, demonized individuals project their lust on an intended victim and demon powers go to work to trap that person. Adultery is the result. It is interesting to me how the innocent spouse may attempt to warn their partner of what is happening to them. Yet the spouse, if under a defiling "spell," seems oblivious to the danger. "Projection" is real and a wise person would immediately break off that association before it is too late.

Projection can be misdiagnosed and a false judgment made about the person you are with. So for me, if I am overwhelmed by evil thoughts when I am in the presence of someone, I silently "bind" the spirit off of myself and pray for the person I am with. If they are bound by the power of darkness, my praying could be the beginning of their being set free. However, I always acknowledge the fact that I have a fallen nature that I am responsible for controlling. It may not necessarily be another person projecting on me. So, I will repent for those thoughts as well.

A fourth way that relationships spread defilement is through what I call an "archetypal" defilement. The relationship is impersonal in nature and defilement is spread community wide, nation-wide, or globally. A good case in point would be Adolph Hitler in Germany who, as the head of government, and himself demonized, took the position of power at his disposal to defile a nation with racism, foolish pride, hatred, and the murdering of six million Jews as well as millions of other innocent people.

Another fascinating example is MTV which has now become a worldwide phenomenon. I was in New Zealand a few years ago and turned on the television only to be greeted with MTV. The same is true in Singapore, Russia, and many other nations I have visited. A whole generation of young people has been raised up on the defilement communicated through the music and images of this popular form of entertainment. Defilement, through various forms of media, has dramatically affected the way we think. Things that were seen as evil are now accepted as the norm. An example of this is a survey I came across a few years ago in the American Family Association Journal on the subject of homosexuality. In 1991, only 17% of teens surveyed were comfortable with homosexuality. In 1999, the same survey was conducted and 54% of the teens were comfortable with homosexuality. In eight short years, a practice seen for generations as evil is now accepted as normal by a majority of teens. Defilement has spread dramatically.

4

The Touch of Evil

The second way defilement spreads is through exposure to evil. This can take place in two ways; vicariously and directly through personally being hurt. Let's look at the vicarious exposure to evil. What I mean by vicarious evil is that the person does not commit the evil himself, but watches it being done by someone else. A person is vicariously exposed to evil through someone else's act. An incident that happened in my family is a good example. After raising four boys my mom decided to go back to school and get a degree in child psychology. The only recipient of this training was my little sister who was in grade school at the time. We would tease my mom that if she had gotten her degree earlier we would not have gotten all those spankings. In order to get her degree she had to enroll in a abnormal psychology class. One assignment was to read a particular book that told of horrible crimes committed by psychologically deranged people. One day while reading this book she felt herself sinking into a dark deep pit and the Holy Spirit spoke to her to stop reading the book and remove herself from the class. She obeyed. What others had done was defiling her as she read about their deeds. The Holy Spirit protected her.

One of the primary ways vicarious evil is defiling people is through the media's fascination with pornography and gratuitous violence. These are tools in the enemy's arsenal to defile. The one who observes others doing evil or portraying it mistakenly justifies himself with the thought that he is not personally involved in the evil activity, but only watching or playing a role. He deceives himself in thinking he is exempt from the evil. This is not the case. One is participating in the evil when one's gratification of lust is the focus. Even in a court of law, if you witness a crime being done to another and do not do anything about it, you can be seen as an accessory to the crime, culpable for aiding and abetting. Demons who are the most legalistic entities in the universe, will push for their rights to afflict a person on the same basis.

We live in a time when pornography has become big business. The internet has become a goldmine for pornography. In fact, some have said that the internet is empowered by the porn business. It is as though a sewer pipeline from hell has been opened to pour defilement into homes around the world. Never before has lust had such access to so many people's minds. The tragedy is that vile images, once planted in a mind, are hard to remove and they can affect one's orientation of reality. Keep in mind, if the problem is not dealt with, the pollution can so permeate one's mind that it leads to demonization. As I have already stated, defilement is the precursor, a preliminary stage for demonization. As such, internet porn is a primary mechanism for the demonization of our society.

There is a solution to being exposed to evil vicariously and that is to fight. Choose not to participate and if need be, expose the evil or embarrass it. From time to time, I have opportunity to travel to minister in other places in the United States and foreign nations. I attempt to travel with my wife or a businessman in my church to protect myself from yielding to defilement. I am convinced that demonic powers work hard to create scenarios that would defile us as I shared in the introduction. On one occasion while I was visiting one of our extension churches, I arrived in my hotel around 11:00pm and was waiting for my assistant pastor to pick me up to go out for a very late dinner. I had about twenty minutes to wait so I decided to turn the television on. This particular hotel was on satellite and for some reason the scrambler which blocked out pornographic programming did not work properly. When I turned the channels, I was confronted with fuzzy pornographic images. I quickly turned off the television. I did not want Satan to have any advantage over me, so when the pastor picked me up, I immediately told him what had happened. After dinner when I returned to my room, the Holy Spirit gave me clear instructions that while I was staying in that hotel I was not to turn on the television. I obeyed.

Another way exposure to evil causes defilement is when we are personally touched by evil which results in being hurt. My wife and I were driving home one afternoon. Colleen was at the wheel. Although she was driving the speed limit an impatient man behind her kept riding her back bumper. She was not able to speed up or move over immediately. Finally, there was an opening and she pulled over. As he passed he gave her an obscene gesture. Colleen got so angry, she screamed out, "God, just kill him." I was stunned. She fumed all the way home and continued on after we had been home for some time. I could not understand her feelings. This was not her usual action. The thought quickened in my mind that she had been defiled. Believing this thought was from the Lord I said to Colleen, "I believe you have been defiled." I laid my hands upon her and prayed over her, commanding the defilement to be broken in Jesus name. If I had not seen it personally, I would not have believed it. My wife instantly changed. The anger lifted and she was back to herself. Her hurt allowed the anger of that man to defile her. Another instance was when my wife attended a women's prayer group. One of the participants shared how she was having recurring nightmares that would wake her up in sheer terror. Colleen shared the story with me and asked what she should do about it. I knew that this lady suffered through a particularly hard situation with an unfaithful husband. I wondered, could she have been defiled from the hurt caused by her husband's sin? I said, "Colleen, at the next meeting pray over her and deal with the defilement." That is what she did and the woman did not have the nightmares anymore. In my book, <u>Closing the Forbidden Door</u>, I mention how unhealed trauma can be an open door for demonic power to control one's life. It is therefore not unusual to see defilement work in this way as a tool of the enemy to move the person into a greater position of bondage.

5

Be Careful of the "Stuff" and the "Digs"

A third way Satan attempts to defile is through defiled objects (stuff) or places (digs). In *Acts 19* we read of God doing extra ordinary miracles through the Apostle Paul. In *verse 12*, it states, *"so that even handkerchiefs and aprons that had touched him were taken to the sick, and their illnesses were cured and the evil spirits left them."* I interpret this to mean that the anointing, the work of the Holy Spirit that flowed through Paul, was transferred via the handkerchiefs and aprons and were effective for the healing of the sick and the deliverance of the demonized. A similar situation is found in *Mark 5:25-34*, when the woman who had been hemorrhaging for a long time believed if she would but touch the hem of Jesus' garment she would be healed. Now, could not the same principle be at work in the realm of the demonic? In fact, idolatry is based upon the pagan concept common to all animists that certain objects have a power residing in them. Given the fact that demons do exist and do desire to control people by any means, it would not seem strange that certain objects could be used by demonic powers as a means of exerting influence over people. This would be especially true if the person put their faith into that object.

I found this to be the case in my own experience and other people I know. Years ago while in graduate school I made it a practice to always buy something for my wife on my return home from a two week intense study leave. On one occasion I brought home what my wife wanted, a set of dishes. On one trip my wife requested I bring her home some lingerie. I felt embarrassed walking into the store to buy the items, but I dutifully fulfilled my wife's request. The next day while studying I became overwhelmed by sexual thoughts. On inquiring of the Lord about the problem I was impressed to pray over the gift I had bought for my wife. It occurred to me that when I was in the store there was a number of teenage girls all buying similar items. The thought struck me: what if the manufacturer had specifically designed and marketed this lingerie for the purpose of eliciting lust? These girls apparently were using the items for the purpose of seduction, but could it be that without knowing it, the objects themselves were seducing them to evil? I took the objects I purchased and prayed over them, breaking any defilement off of them. It was like the difference between night and day. The oppression lifted immediately. I was so shocked by the freedom I felt, I struggled to believe it really happened. The experience which took place around twenty years ago made it clear to me there were spiritual forces at work within certain objects.

Others have expressed similar situations. C. Peter Wagner shared how he was in a hotel room attempting to prepare for a lecture by spending some time in prayer. However, he found it extremely difficult to pray. It was as though there was evil in the room which overwhelmed him. Feeling prompted by the Lord, he went into the restroom. While standing in front of the mirror he again felt prompted to pull open a drawer and reach his hand way to the back of it. He felt something and pulled it out. It was a vile pornographic magazine. He immediately took it out of his room and threw the magazine into the dumpster. The moment he walked back into the room the atmosphere had changed. The spiritual fog had lifted and he was able to pray and prepare for his meeting.

Another incident happened through the ministry of James Robison, a popular evangelist. A businessman in Dallas who had acquired numerous art objects happened to show them to James Robison. He commented to the businessman that these objects were idols. The owner decided to destroy them and in so doing the businessman's wife immediately experienced the lifting of an oppression she had felt while living in that house. The fact the owner would destroy what to some were very costly art objects made the news in Dallas-Ft. Worth papers.

I am convinced that defiled objects affect more Christians than we know. Let's suppose before you were a Christian you had a relationship with a person and sexual sin was committed. Suppose you still keep objects acquired during that relationship. Could those objects possibly be seen as defiled objects since they remind you of and tie you to the sinful relationship? The object may be a ring, letters, clothing, or some memento, yet they can take on the status of an idol if one is not careful. Praying for guidance from the Holy Spirit will bring revelation of what to do with such items.

Some objects not only are defiling, but they carry curses with them. These curses can give demons rights to afflict or manifest themselves. In Dr. Kenneth McAll's book entitled, <u>Healing the Family Tree</u>, he tells the story of a woman by the name of Muriel who came to see him. He described her as very pale, depressed, and confused. Since Dr. McAll was a medical doctor he examined her and found out she was anemic with low blood pressure. She complained about seeing little black dots. Dr. McAll prayed for her and as he did the Holy Spirit said, "Ask her about the walking stick." Shocked that someone would ask her she began to unravel her very unusual story. She said, "Nobody knows this, but in the floorboard of my house is a jewel-encrusted walking stick worth thousands of dollars that my ancestors, generations before, stole from another family. It is in a special compartment in my house under the floor." Dr. McAll said, "You know you have to give that back." She researched and discovered the family that once owned this particular walking stick and gave it back to the distant relative of the original owner. Two weeks after she returned the stick, every problem she had physically was gone. [7]

---

7   Kenneth McAll, <u>Healing the Family Tree</u>. (England: Sheldon Press, 1985) 71&72. (book out of print)

A similar incident of such a defiled object affected a family in my church. I was called to the house because of demonic manifestations that were affecting the whole household. I was impressed by the Holy Spirit to ask a question of the wife. It was, "Do you have any objects given to you by a witch doctor?" To her husband's surprise she said, "Yes." She had received a special potion from a witch doctor in the Philippines and kept it hidden for many years. I suggested it would be a great idea to get rid of the object so we took it, broke it, and buried it.

Dr. McAll tells a story similar about a Methodist minister whose four year old son, John, had epileptic-type seizures. In talking to the father he discovered that this Methodist minister had a spiritualist friend for over fifteen years. This friend had given him a large amount of occultic material which the minister had been studying. Dr. McAll, shocked that a minister would be reading such material, said, "When you seek forgiveness from God and burn these books, your son will be healed. You're a Methodist minister and you're breaking God's laws." At that, the Methodist minister got so angry with Dr. McAll he threw him out of his house. However, a short time later his son went into a tremendous number of fits that lasted for over thirty-six hours. In desperation his Methodist preacher father ran to a church nearby, repented of his sins before the pastor, and burned all his occult books. From that moment on his son John never had another attack again. It is important that every Christian cleanse their home or work place from anything that could be a source of defilement. In *Acts 19:18-19*, Christians confessed their evil deeds, brought their sorcery scrolls, and burned them publicly; stuff valued over five million dollars in today's money. They did this because a holy fear convinced them to rid themselves of anything that was used by Satan to bind them or render them defiled.

Not only are objects defiled, but places can be defiled and affect people that stay there. This is seen in *Leviticus 14*, where a place was seen as defiled in much the same way a leprous man is defined as defiled. My wife and I had been married for about two years when we bought our first home. It was the perfect place for us and God did a number of miracles for us just to be able to buy it. After we moved in I noticed that my wife was feeling very lonely when she stayed in the house. One day she called me and said, "Honey, I think something is wrong with this house. I believe there is a spirit in this house." So I came home and we both prayed, commanded the spirit to leave, and blessed the house. The change was immediate and she no longer felt lonely. The house we had purchased had been owned by a widow. Her husband had died in the house and she lived alone in that house for many years. I believe her grief attracted a spirit of loneliness that stayed in the house even after the owner had moved out. That spirit only left when it was forcefully ejected by prayer in the name of Jesus.

For further insight into this subject of demons attached to places, let me recommend my first book on spiritual warfare, <u>You Can Be a Winner in the Invisible War: The Power of Binding and Loosing</u>, as well as George Otis, Jr.'s book, <u>The Twilight Labyrinth</u>.

We have seen three ways – I call these passageways – that Satan uses to bring defilement: through relationships, being touched by evil either vicariously or personally, and finally through defiled objects or places. But, how do we live free of defilement? That is the subject of the final chapters.

6

The Blood Brotherhood

The book of *I John* specifically speaks to our defiled generation. *I John 1:5-7,* is especially relevant to answering the question, "how do we stay free of defilement?" The passage states: *"This is the message we have heard from him and declare to you: God is light; in him there is no darkness at all. If we claim to have fellowship with him yet walk in the darkness, we lie and do not live by the truth. But if we walk in the light, as he is in the light, we have fellowship with one another, and the blood of Jesus, his Son, purifies us from all sin."*

The cleansing agent to all sin and all defilement is the "blood of Jesus." The blood represents Jesus' life being poured out as the perfect, "once and for all" sacrifice for our sin.[8] It is no wonder that the church is pictured in *Revelation 7:14*, as those who have *"washed their robes and made them white in the blood of the Lamb."*

The writer of Hebrews shows the power of Christ's blood by saying, *"The blood of goats and bulls and the ashes of a heifer sprinkled on those who are ceremonially unclean sanctify them so that they are outwardly clean. How much more, then, will the blood of Christ, who, through the eternal Spirit offered himself unblemished to God, cleanse our consciences from acts that lead to death, so that we may serve the living God!"* *(Hebrews 9:13-14)* The writer of Hebrews goes on to make the point that the *"Law requires that nearly everything be cleansed with blood, and without the shedding of blood there is no forgiveness."* *(Hebrews 9:22)*

This emphasis on blood seems so foreign to the twenty-first century person because sacrifices are not an everyday occurrence. The best picture for us to understand the significance of Christ's blood is found in the Old Testament story of the first Passover. God was in the

8   Refer to I Peter 3:18: "For Christ died for sins once for all, the righteous for the unrighteous, to bring you to God." Hebrews 7:27: "He sacrificed for their sins once for all when he offered himself."

process of delivering Israel out of Egypt. The final plague that God sent which ultimately released them was the killing of the first-born sons and the first-born of the cattle. (*Exodus 11:4-8, 12:1-30*) In order for someone to be spared from this plague, they had to kill a year old male lamb without defect and take its blood and apply it to the top and two sides of the outside door-post of the house. When the death angel passed by, those living in the house where the blood had been applied were spared. *Exodus 12:13* states, *"The blood will be a sign for you on the houses where you are; and when I see the blood, I will pass over you. No destructive plague will touch you when I strike Egypt."* It is not by accident that Jesus was crucified during the Passover season because He fulfilled all that Passover really means. For salvation, that is, freedom from sin and eternal life, we must apply the blood of Jesus to the door-post of our heart. We must receive Jesus into our life. We do this by repenting of sin and calling on Jesus to forgive us and be our Lord. (*Romans 10:9-10*) This begins our life in God. However, in *I John 1:7*, the Apostle John emphasizes two things we must do in order to have the blood of Christ continue to purify us.

The first thing we must do is be a part of a fellowship of believers. John writes, *"We have fellowship with one another and the blood of Jesus, his son, purifies us from all sin."*

The same emphasis is found in *I John 1:3*, *"We proclaim to you what we have seen and heard, so that you also may have fellowship with us. And our fellowship is with the Father and with his Son, Jesus Christ."* The key word is fellowship. Salvation is individual, yet it is lived out in community.

The reason this is so is because when God made us as human beings, He gave us the capacity to love. Love itself creates an innate need for fellowship. Even though Adam could express his love to God, it was God who said, "It is not good for man to be alone." Our love relationship with God is also expressed through our love for others. Love cannot exist in a vacuum; it is learned through our interaction with others.

This becomes even more crucial as we now must cope with our fallen-ness. We are innately selfish. When Christ comes into our lives He gives us a new nature like Himself – the Holy Spirit is at work in us to conform us into His image. Yet whether we like it or not we must contend with our old nature until we die. At times we walk in the Holy Spirit and crucify the flesh, but then there are times when the enemy of our soul tries to shock our fallen human nature back to life through defilement. The local church is a holy brotherhood that helps to protect us from this. I call it the "blood brotherhood," for we have all been linked together by the "blood of Christ." Being committed to a local church allows us to have God speak into our lives on a consistent basis. We are supported in developing godly disciplines of regularly praying, giving, fasting, etc. The local church provides opportunity to serve and receive a corresponding working of God's Spirit in a special way. Most of all, the church allows us to have accountability, especially when we are in a small group. All of these things protect us from defilement.

One might say, "I do not need to be in a church. I can get my spiritual feeding through books, television, and other media forms available today." The greatest problem is that we can be locked in a particular way of thinking which can only be changed by real interaction with others.

Recently one of my ministers on staff commented about a person who was involved in our church, yet when they got to actually voicing what they were thinking, this staff minister realized that some of their thinking was distorted. As they interacted it became apparent that this person needed time with someone to sort through some of the issues that caused the distortion. This takes personal time, but it is time well spent for we are bearing one another's burdens, and so fulfilling the law of Christ. (*Galatians 6:2*)

I believe in the heart of every true Christian there is a God-given desire to be a part of a church, the "blood fellowship." I know this was true for me.

As a seventeen year old young man, I graduated from high school in the Philippines where my parents were missionaries. In order to get back to the United States and to have some money for college, I worked myself across the Pacific on an American freighter that was unloading cargo in Vietnam. God proved Himself to me on that trip and how He did is worthy of a book itself. However, being seventeen years old on a ship of hardened perverts was very challenging. One seaman had contracted VD twelve times. Although many of them had families at home, they lived and worked for the next port where they would drink and fornicate. Some had favorite girls in each port. It was disgusting and it weighed heavily on my soul. I was thankful for my strong Christian upbringing and a family praying for me. I did not yield to the sexual pressure and remained pure. But, one of the things I longed for was Christian fellowship. I would take my ukulele and sing praises to God at the back of the ship when I was not working. Then at every port we landed I would seek out a church to worship in. Two incidents stand out. Our ship had arrived in Vietnam in the middle of a war zone. It was a Wednesday evening and after work I took a ferry in to shore to look for a church to worship in. It was raining and since I had no transportation I hitchhiked. The driver of an American military jeep graciously dropped me off at the military chapel where an American chaplain was holding a worship service. I was sopping wet. I sat all the way in the back so I would not disturb the service in progress. I was cold so I grabbed newspapers from a shelf and put them under my wet shirt to stay warm. The service lasted less than an hour. I do not even remember what the chaplain preached about, but I was in church! I hitchhiked back to the pier only to be notified that because of sniper fire the ferry had shut down and would not resume until morning. I had no place to stay. Still wet, I crouched under a shed that seemed unoccupied. I lay down on the floor and prayed that I would wake to see another day. In the middle of a war zone, unarmed and alone, there was no guarantee I would make it, but I did.

The second incident that took place was when our ship stopped in Yokohama, Japan for repairs. It was Sunday and I longed to be in church. I found out there was a Christian church so I hired a taxi to take me there. Little did I know it was all the way on the other side of the city. I used all my money to pay for the taxi. When I arrived, it was a house with about twenty to thirty people sitting on the floor. The entire service was in Japanese; however communion was served and just worshipping with my brothers and sisters, even though I did not understand the language, fed my soul. I had no way to get back to my ship since I had no money, but through the kindness of my Japanese brothers and sisters in Christ, they put me in a cab and paid the fare.

At every stop during that trip I sought out a church. It did not matter what it cost me I was going to worship with the family of God. There was a cleansing and refreshing that took place when I was there. In *I Timothy 4:5*, the Apostle Paul states, *"It is consecrated by the word of God and prayer."* In the context he is talking about food, yet I found the same principle at work in the process of cleansing from defilement; being among the people of God where the Word of God was preached and prayers were lifted to God. Because of my experience, it is hard for me to understand how people can say they love Jesus, but do not go to church. I longed to be in the house of the Lord and still do. The desire to be a part of the local church, the "blood brotherhood," is essential in living free of defilement.

That brings us to the second part of *I John 1:7*, *"If we walk in the light, as he is in the light."* There are certain things we must do to stay free of defilement. That is the subject of the remainder of the book.

7

The Power of Confession

"For you were once darkness, but now you are light in the Lord. Live as children of light (for the fruit of the light consists in all goodness, righteousness and truth) and find out what pleases the Lord. Have nothing to do with the fruitless deeds of darkness, but rather expose them. For it is shameful even to mention what the disobedient do in secret. But everything exposed by the light becomes visible." (Ephesians 5:8-13) This text seems to indicate that we cannot keep any deep dark secret in our life, any evil unexposed sin, for it will be like a cancer which can destroy us. The Apostle Paul's argument

is clear. He has just talked about being imitators of God and being holy people where there should not be even *"a hint of sexual immorality or of any kind of impurity or of greed." (verse 3)* Even what we talk about should not be tainted with evil. His point is, we are children of light and as such we can no longer live in darkness or allow what is darkness to find any place in us. But how do we keep living in the light when we are surrounded by such darkness? We know that due to our fallen nature, darkness tends to find easy access into our lives. *Verse 13* gives the answer. I like how the New King James version states it. *"But all things that are exposed are made manifest by the light, for whatever makes manifest is light."* As we confess the evil, it no longer has a hold on us. No longer is it a hook for the enemy to control our lives with. When we confess our sins we are free because the darkness "becomes light." The only reason this can happen is because Jesus, *"the light,"* has come into the world and through His sacrificial death on the cross and resurrection conquered sin and death. He has the power to forgive us and turn darkness to light. That is why the Apostle John can write, *"If we confess our sins, he is faithful and just and will forgive us our sins and purify us from all unrighteousness." (I John 1:9)* In fact, the Apostle John uses the same picture of light and darkness in *I John 1:5-8, 2:7-11*. We lie if we say we are Christians, followers of Jesus who is the light, yet we do things that are of the darkness. Confession is crucial and because of what Christ did for us we can be forgiven. But, what is fascinating is how this cleansing of Christ's blood works. It works within the context of the church – "fellowship with one another" – as we have just seen in the previous chapter. Yes, Jesus forgives us individually when we confess our sins to Him, when we repent, and receive Him as Lord, but there is an ongoing work of his forgiveness within the context of our being a part of a "fellowship." We were never meant to be lone rangers. It is here that we see the importance of James' insight in *James 5:16*. He states, *"Therefore confess your sins to each other and pray for each other so that you may be healed."* He says this within the context of the church's healing ministry. Clearly James sees confession as a part of the healing process. Some have suggested that here James uses a different word in the original Greek language than what is used for sin and instead should be translated, faults. As we confess our faults we can experience true healing. I am convinced certain sicknesses are the result of being defiled and our open confession is the means by which healing can be released.

Who we confess to is important. A false theology emerged in the church that came to fruition during the middle ages that a certain group of church people were mediators between God and man. They took the title, "priests," an Old Testament word for mediator. So, you told your sins to a priest and on God's behalf he forgave you. Although the act of confession was right, the theology was wrong. When one becomes a Christian, one has become mystically a part of Christ's body. He is the true priest, the one mediator, so all of us in essence are priests. We all have the same right to come boldly into God's presence because of what Jesus Christ did and ask for what we need. *(Hebrews 4:16)*

Then who do we confess to? Start with those who you have offended. Who has your selfishness affected the most? For example, if you lied, ask for forgiveness from the person you lied to. Let's suppose you watched pornography and you are a married man. You need to confess and ask forgiveness from your wife because you have attempted to have sexual gratification outside of your marriage commitment. In so doing the enemy of your soul has distorted the true picture of sexuality in your mind and caused your wife to be demeaned by your activity. If you are not married, then maybe you can confess to a men's group that you are accountable to, a friend you feel you can confide in, or your pastor. Keep in mind – whatever is hidden Satan will use to manipulate your life with.

A case in point is a married couple I counseled who were having extreme problems with anger in their marriage. In close examination I discovered that the man had committed adultery earlier in their marriage, but had never told his wife. His wife suspected something but when confronted he would lie. To make matters worse, he would project on his wife the very sin he committed, accusing her of adultery and exhibiting an insane jealousy. The marriage fell apart. What happened was the very thing he feared; the break up of his marriage. That fear prevented him from confessing his sin to his wife, but in the end his hiding of his sin produced actions and attitudes in him that led to the breakup of the marriage anyway. Satan does not play fair. He tempts us, and when we yield he condemns us, and then prevents us from getting healed by causing us to be afraid to confess. I have often wondered what the end result would have been if he had confessed earlier. Now, I am not suggesting that we unload our guilt by just confessing everything we have done without being sensitive to the weight we are placing on those we have confessed to. Timing and sensitivity to the Holy Spirit's prompting is important. There are those our confession can cause great grief and damage to. However, we must keep in mind that as long as something is hidden in our lives, it gives a power base to Satan to manipulate us, condemn us, and keep us in a state of defilement. Why did Jesus make a big point of the woman with the issue of blood touching Him? Yes, He felt power leave Him and he said, *"Who touched me?"*

However, the woman who touched him was classified as defiled by the law and it was a serious crime in her state to touch someone for she would render them unclean. Jesus' recognition of her was a validation of her faith as well as declaring to all that she was cleansed – no longer defiled. Her secret had to come out in the open.

In my marriage, I am one with my wife; she is my closest confidant and protection from defilement. If I have seen something, said something, or did something that was not right, I would confess it to her. Her openness to forgive, understand, encourage, and correct, not only frees me, but draws us closer to each other. I could not imagine carrying the weight of ministry without having my wife with me. It has never been easy to humble myself and confess my failures or ask forgiveness. Ego is always a major stumbling block for all of us. However, I have attempted to make confession and asking for forgiveness a lifestyle which has found expression, not only in my marriage, but in my family and in my work. Many times I have sought forgiveness from my children or a staff member when I have wronged them. Jesus commanded us to do this. In *Matthew 5:23-24,* He said, *"Therefore, if you are offering your gift at the altar and there remember that your brother has something against you, leave your gift there in front of the altar. First go and be reconciled to your brother; then come and offer your gift."* If we are to be cleansed of defilement we must do this.

Coupled with confession must be repentance. Repentance reflects an attitude of brokenness, a painful awareness of our sinfulness and desperate need of God's forgiveness. It also reflects a desire to change, to be willing to do whatever is needed to be done in order to live right. Some have suggested true repentance is an about-face, going one way and turning one hundred-eighty degrees to go the other way. I am convinced that true repentance goes hand in hand with confession. Inward change and outward confession are keys to salvation and to breaking the power of defilement. The Apostle Paul writes, *"For it is with your heart that you believe and are justified, and it is with your mouth that you confess and are saved."* (Romans 10:10)

The second person we must confess to is to the person who has hurt us. I call this confrontation. Jesus commands us to do this in *Matthew 18:15*: *"If your brother sins against you, go and show him his fault, just between the two of you. If he listens to you, you have won your brother over."* Jesus goes on to say that if they do not repent, take one or two others along to confront them, and if they still do not repent, then bring it to the church. There is much in this passage on how this process can be a way the offender can be healed. But, looking at it from the perspective of the person who has been offended, hurt, and defiled, it can provide a clear means of healing.

Let's look at this from a number of viewpoints. First, the desire for justice is a part of being made in the image of God. Often anger is a response to injustice and motivates a person to do something to seek justice. However, if not handled correctly, anger can provide a place from which the devil can operate out of a person's life. The Apostle Paul writes in *Ephesians 4:26-27*, *"In your anger do not sin.' Do not let the sun go down while you are still angry, and do not give the devil a foothold."* Unresolved anger leads to vengeance and bitterness which defiles us and makes us a fountain of defilement on those around us. Therefore, confronting those who have hurt us helps provide others with the opportunity to repent and ask forgiveness or at least inform them how deeply they hurt us and in so doing give release to our entrapped anger.

Sometimes out of an attempt to protect ourselves from further pain we do not confront. We keep it all a secret. However, the problem is that there is no justice and it affects our thinking, moving us to a distorted picture of ourselves and others.

Years ago a man in our church shared with me in counseling how as a boy he was raped by his friend's dad. Justice was never done and the incident left him feeling that something must be wrong with him. He ended up living a homosexual life-style, a distorted sexual orientation. Although we as Christians must leave vengeance to God and to civil authorities, it is our job to confront, to bring our hurt into the open so that justice is possible and defilement from the incident is able to be cleansed.

A grandmother asked me for some advice. Her two grandchildren had been sexually abused by a relative who lived in their home. He was arrested and her question was whether the children should go to court. My advice was that they needed to see their tormentor publicly confronted and brought to justice. They also needed to hear him apologize to them. On the basis of my counsel she did just what I said. Their molester did apologize publicly, he was convicted, and they saw him leave in shackles to start his sentence in jail. Although very young, they needed to know justice had been done and an apology was made. The grandmother said the parents reported a definite healing taking place in the children. They began to act like normal children again.

Confrontation, as we've seen, can begin the process of healing, however, confrontation has another aspect to it. We are finite. Only God knows everything. We do not. Therefore, we may think we understand something and make judgments, only to find how wrong we are. We may not know how distorted perceptions are until we confront those who we think hurt us. Recently a person confessed to me how angry they were that they had not been given the right information from some company worker concerning a particular task they were to do. This person had interpreted misinformation as a lack of respect for her. This led her to think they were purposely withholding from her so she would fail in doing her job. However, when she confronted one of the co-workers she found out her perspective was completely wrong. They were not keeping information from her. They were as ignorant as she was about the task and just like her, only got the information they needed when they attempted to do the task. The affect this revelation had on the offended party was amazing. She had become angry, which produced a self-loathing, a desire to no longer work in her occupation and resentment against her co-workers, all on false assumptions. The perceived injustice was corrected when she confronted the person.

How thankful I am that years ago someone who I offended confronted me about my actions. I was a singles pastor on retreat with a large group of singles. One of the singles came to me and said, "Why don't you like me?" I did not understand. He proceeded to tell me that he had said, "Hi!" to me and I didn't even acknowledge him. His comment caused me to become acutely aware of a weakness

I have. I tend to get so caught up in things that I become oblivious to what people around me are doing. When I shared with him my weakness, asked him to forgive me, and assured him I did like him, he was healed and that realization helped me to be more conscious of how I offend others by my actions. But I have often thought: What if he had not confronted me? He may have gone through life feeling rejected by me. Now, I am not going to psycho-analyze all the potential fallout of this, but it is clear it could have had a defiling affect on him, though I was innocent of any desire to hurt him. Because of our limited understanding, his confrontation blessed us both.

Finally, in regard to confession, is there a time when I don't need to confront? Some people, due to their sensitive nature, are always feeling hurt by someone and they would wind up being consumed by the task of confronting everyone and in the process become extremely self-centered. What one could do is to look objectively at the hurt by asking certain questions: Does it only affect me or is there a probability this has been done to others, if not now, in the future? Is the information going to help or hinder the person in their relationship with Christ? How does God view what they did? How have I been affected by the hurt? Is it something I can overlook by a God-given grace? How badly does it bother me? Has an injustice been done? The Apostle Peter states, *"Above all, love each other deeply, because love covers over a multitude of sins." (I Peter 4:8)*

There are times I have shared my hurt with my wife, who helps me see it differently. There are times in prayer God will tell me not to make an issue of it, to simply forgive and He will take care of it. The bottom line is that we must be sensitive to the Holy Spirit for He will lead us. I have found that if the hurt continues to affect me and is not getting healed, then it is one way God is saying to me that I need to expose and confront it.

8

Pray Through

When I was growing up one of the spiritual catch phrases was "pray through." It meant to seek God until you got the assurance of answered prayer. Because defilement is a demonic attack upon us, prayer is not only our weapon through which the Holy Spirit works, but our protective canopy and means of healing. Let me explain. Prayer for the Christian should be a lifestyle. The Apostle Paul writes, *"Pray without ceasing." (I Thessalonians 5:17 – KJV)* When we look at the prayer life of the Apostle Paul we see a man committed to prayer. He encourages each of the churches he writes to by declaring his fervent prayer for them. In fact, the Apostle Paul states to the Thessalonica church, *"Night and day we pray most earnestly." (I Thessalonians 3:10)* He writes the same thing to Timothy, *"Night and day I constantly remember you in my prayers." (II Timothy 1:3)* Our biggest problem, at least in American churches, is that prayer is an occasional religious activity, not a passion, nor a lifestyle. Therefore, the power of evil tends to have a greater sway on our culture than it should. We are not using the means at our disposal to stop the enemy's defiling work. Prayer must be something we do consistently, daily, night and day. In our prayers we must ask the Lord to protect us, to reveal anything in us that is not right. We must pray to be filled with His Spirit. The Apostle Paul declares, *"So I say, live by the Spirit, and you will not gratify the desires of the sinful nature." (Galatians 5:16)*

In his book How Long will God Wait?, author T. Dale Pollard shares his testimony of how, under an "academic umbrella" he became hooked on pornography. In a time of desperation for relief from this bondage he repented, crying for over an hour. He states, "The transforming work of the Holy Spirit brought miracles into my life. Perhaps the greatest was my almost immediate realization that there was strength within me greater than the pull of fleshly desires. My sexual desire, which had seemed insatiable and untamable, was now manageable. Pornography lost its grip."[9] He prayed through and was set free.

Our praying can have a dramatic affect for others as well. A little four year old girl had been sexually abused, but the diligent prayers by her family and their friends made a difference. One day she told her mother this amazing story. After the abuse she would see a "monster in her eyes," but one evening she had a dream. In the dream she saw Jesus come and kill the monster. She woke up the next morning singing and dancing, and told her mother that she no longer sees the monster anymore.

We must not only pray, but also have others pray for us. If I have been defiled I have found the best way to be cleansed is to repent, confess and have someone lay hands on me, praying and breaking the defilement. The laying on of hands is basic to the Christian life as the writer of Hebrews mentions in *Hebrews 6:2*. It can be an act of healing, blessing, infilling of the Spirit, and impartation. I thought it interesting that oil and blood were applied to the person who was once defiled by leprosy and now seen as clean. To me it is a picture of the work of Christ on the cross to cleanse and the work of the Holy Spirit to empower the believer. The Apostle Paul writes, *"He saved us through the washing of rebirth and renewal by the Holy*

9   T. Dale Pollard, How Long Will God Wait? (Ardmore, Oklahoma: Healing Hurting Hearts Ministries) 239.

Spirit." (Titus 3:5) One cannot keep clean or be cleansed without the work of the Holy Spirit. He convicts us of sin, and His gifts, when ministered to us, bring encouragement, discernment, healing, the prophetic, and much more. Prayer releases the work of the Holy Spirit in our lives and in others. That is why the Apostle Paul sees it as a weapon against the enemy and encourages us to pray *"on all occasions." (Ephesians 6:13-18)*

9

Renew Your Mind With the Word

If we are to live free of defilement we must not only practice true confession and prayer, but we must also live in God's Word. The second part of the Apostle Paul's exhortation in *Ephesians 6*, is the word of God. *"Take...the sword of the Spirit, which is the Word of God. And pray."* In fact, the Apostle Paul sees the church being cleansed and made holy by the Word. *"To make her holy, cleansing her by the washing with water through the word." (Ephesians 5:26)* In *II Timothy 3:16* we read, *"All scriptures are God-breathed and is useful for teaching, rebuking, correcting and training in righteousness...*" The Word of God is like a compass - it keeps you on course or gets you back on track. We must not only read the Word for ourselves, but sit under the Word being preached.

Scriptures talk so much about the difference between the Christian and the world, between the flesh and the spirit. Without our knowing it we can become defiled by the world. The Bible warns us not to love the world or the things in the world, for if one does, love for God will disappear. *(I John 2:15)* There are lists in scripture to help us have a spiritual check-up so that this does not happen.

One such list is found in *I Corinthians 6:9-11*. *"Do you not know that the wicked will not inherit the kingdom of God? Do not be deceived: Neither the sexually immoral nor idolators nor adulterers nor male prostitutes nor homosexual offenders nor thieves nor the greedy nor drunkards nor slanderers nor swindlers will inherit the kingdom of God. And that is what some of you were. But you were washed, you were sanctified, you were justified in the name of the Lord Jesus Christ and by the Spirit of our God."*

Another list, as was cited in Chapter 2, is in *Galatians 5:19-21*. *"The acts of the sinful nature are obvious: sexual immorality, impurity and debauchery; idolatry and witchcraft; hatred, discord, jealousy, fits of rage, selfish ambition, dissensions, factions and envy; drunkenness, orgies, and the like. I warn you, as I did before, that those who live like this will not inherit the kingdom of God."* In *Romans 1:18*, the Apostle Paul talks about the wrath of God. He makes it clear that if a Christian does the things mentioned they are deceived. They will not go to heaven, but to hell for they will experience God's wrath. They suppress truth by their wickedness and God gives them up to their passions and to a depraved mind. Paul goes on to make a list of *"wickedness, evil, greed and depravity." He states, "They are full of envy, murder, strife, deceit and malice. They are gossips, slanderers, God-haters, insolent, arrogant and boastful; they invent ways of doing evil; they disobey their parents; they are senseless, faithless, heartless, ruthless." (verses 29-31)*

When we have a physical exam, medical doctors may request that we have an x-ray done. These scriptures, along with other lists of sins in the New Testament, are exactly that. They are spiritual x-rays exposing sinful actions and attitudes. James likens the Word to a mirror that we must look closely at and then not go away forgetting what we saw. We must be doers of the word and not just hearers, lest we become deceived. *(James 1:22-25)*

The Word keeps our thinking straight as to what is right or wrong. The right perspective is crucial. It is a kind of eyesight. Jesus said, *"The eye is the lamp of the body. If your eyes are good, your whole body will be full of light. But if your eyes are bad, your whole body will be full of darkness. If then the light within you is darkness, how great is that darkness!" (Matthew 6:22-23)* The enemy is constantly, through our own fallen human nature and worldly thinking, tempting us to embrace a demonic perspective of life. It is what the serpent did to Eve when he lied to her about God. She believed his lie. A continued reading, hearing and obeying the Word of God keeps our minds washed from the enemy's lies.

In C.S. Lewis' The Silver Chair from The Chronicles of Narnia, we are reminded of the role of the Word of God in a very unique scene. Aslan has just given Jill specific signs she is to follow in order to accomplish her purpose for being in Narnia. Aslan goes on to state, "But first, remember, remember, remember, the Signs. Say them to yourself when you wake in the morning and when you lie down at night, and when you wake in the middle of the night. And whatever strange things may happen to you, let nothing turn your mind from following the Signs."[10]

The story goes on to describe how Jill got so consumed by her desire to fulfill her own needs that she did not obey Aslan's commands. Her repentance and Aslan's mercy got her back on track in fulfilling her purposes for being in Narnia.

10   C.S. Lewis, The Silver Chair (New York: Collier Books, Macmillan Publishing Company, 1970) 21.

The Word of God reminds us who we are. We are members of God's family. It also reminds us of what we are doing here. As Christians in this world we are reflecting His light. To do this, we are being conformed into the image of Christ. In fact, the Apostle Peter says that God's *"great and precious promises"* help us to *"participate in the divine nature and escape the corruption in the world caused by evil desires."* (*II Peter 1:4*). He goes on to encourage us to *"Make every effort to add to your faith goodness; and to goodness, knowledge; and to knowledge, self-control; and to self-control, perseverance; and to perseverance, godliness; and to godliness, brotherly kindness; and to brotherly kindness, love."* (*II Peter 1:5-7*). These qualities will make the believer more effective and productive and keep them from falling. (*II Peter 1:8*) In a similar way the Apostle Paul tells Timothy four things. First, he is to flee from the love of money. Second, pursue righteousness, godliness, faith, love, endurance, and gentleness. Third, fight the good fight of faith. Finally, he is to take hold of eternal life. (*I Timothy 6:10-12*) In essence, the whole Christian life is being like our Lord, joining in His mission of destroying the works of the devil, seeing the spiritually lost found, becoming His disciples, and advancing His kingdom.

This brings us to our final way of living free of defilement: Guard yourself.

10

Put Your Guard Up

A wise football coach knows that in order to win the football game, he must have a good offense and a good defense. Yes, his team must make points, but they must also stop the other team from scoring. So too the Christian, if he is to live free of defilement, he must have a good defense and guard himself against defilement.

A father asked if I would see his teenage son who was having problems with horrendous sexual thoughts. He attended church and saw himself as a Christian. I agreed to do so. As we prayed at the opening of the session, the Holy Spirit told me to ask a question. "When you were at a friend's house, did you watch a pornographic video?" Shocked, the boy said yes and proceeded to share about the incident. Sadly the boy's father knew nothing about it.

This case and thousands more reinforce the truth that parents must be vigilant as to where their children are and with whom. As we have already noted, Satan does not play fair. He takes advantage of the vulnerable and those who foolishly tread into his domain. We must guard ourselves and those whom we are responsible for. As a parent we must check out whether we protect our children from the three passageways Satan uses to defile – relationships, experiencing evil vicariously or personally, and defiled objects.

I have discovered three specific scriptures that have helped to guard me from defilement. The first is *Matthew 5:30, "If your right hand causes you to sin, cut it off and throw it away. It is better for you to lose one part of your body than for your whole body to go into hell."* This passage makes it clear that hell is so bad that it would be better to go through life maimed than to go there. What is being said is that we are to eliminate anything out of our lives that would tempt us to sin. If it is a relationship, then cut it off. If it is a television or an internet connection or a particular activity, then it must go.

I remember a young man at a youth camp that asked to see me. As we were walking to a place to talk privately, the Holy Spirit told me he had a problem with pornography. I told him what his problem was. He was shocked that I knew, and proceeded to tell me his story. Every day after school he would walk home past a drug store where he would enter and look at the pornographic magazines. "I have an answer for your problem," I said. He waited with baited breath for a revelation of profound wisdom. I simply said, "Walk home from school another way." We can protect ourselves by not putting ourselves in the place of temptation. Cut off the activity. The Apostle Paul uses the word, "flee." We are to flee youthful lusts (*II Timothy 2:22*), flee fornication (*I Corinthians 6:18*), flee idolatry (*I Corinthians 10:14*), and flee the love of money (*I Timothy 6:10-11*). Joseph fled from Potiphar's wife who attempted to seduce him (*Genesis 39:6-12*). There is a time to fight and a time to flee. Fleeing spiritually is putting distance between you and the temptation.

The second verse that speaks about protecting ourselves is *Philippians 4:8-9*. *"Finally, brothers, whatever is true, whatever is noble, whatever is right, whatever is pure, whatever is lovely, whatever is admirable – if anything is excellent or praiseworthy – think about such things. Whatever you have learned or received or heard from me, or seen in me*

– *put it into practice. And the God of peace will be with you."*
We are to set our minds on certain things and we are to be
discipled by righteous people. We must make choices as to
what we will hear and who will be our heroes and who we
will follow. Those choices are made every day. The right
choices will be a protection; it is a proactive position.

The third verse is *Mark 6:7*. Jesus sent His disciples
out two by two. Jesus knew His disciples needed
companionship in their work. Much defilement can be
averted by not being alone. However, that person must be
a person who is righteous. Keep in mind that our greatest
temptations often come when we are alone. Teaming up
with someone fights off discouragement and provides
protection against defilement.

Epilogue

One of the most fascinating persons in scripture is the non-Hebrew prophet Balaam, whose story is told in *Numbers 22-24*. He was unquestionably a prophet of God, yet he was killed when Israel defeated the Midianites. All that is told about Balaam in that passage is that when he tried to curse Israel, God would not let him, but God had him bless Israel instead. We do not get the full story until we read *Numbers 31:8 and 16*. Apparently, since he could not get paid by the Moabite and Midian kings for cursing Israel, he decided he could get the money by giving them advice on how they could get God to curse Israel. He advised them to get the Israelites to sin and then God would judge them. His advice was to get the Moabite and Midianite women to seduce the Israelite men to join them in worshipping their god Baal of Peor. That is exactly what happened and Balaam was right; God sent a plague with 24,000 Israelites being killed. Israel would have been wiped out if Phineas, the grandson of Aaron, had not turned away the wrath of God by killing an Israelite man and a Midianite woman, who had openly flaunted their fornication before Israel.

Satan wants to destroy God's people. In order to have the right to do so, all he has to do is cause them to be defiled. He knows the word of God very well.

In *Leviticus 18*, after a catalogue of sexual activities is mentioned, the Lord said to Moses in verse 24 and 25, *"Do not defile yourselves in any of these ways, because this is how the nations that I am going to drive out before you became defiled. Even the land was defiled; so I punished it for its sin, and the land vomited out its inhabitants."*

It has been seven years since the Lord gave me the revelation on defilement. I have preached it on national television, at some of the largest churches in America, and to college students. In those seven years, defilement has become more pervasive than ever in our society. Pornography has infiltrated all of life. The Kaiser Family Foundation Study recently reported that between 1998 and 2005, the percentage of television shows with sexual content grew from 5% to 70% with the number of sex-related scenes on popular teen programs being 6.7 per hour.[11] The laws

---

11   Jennifer C. Kerr, "What's on TV? A lot of sex, report finds," The Maui News The Associated Press., 10 Nov. 2005:   B6.

of God have been replaced by religious symbolisms and a pseudo compassion for felt needs. Indeed, *"every man is righteous in his own eyes"* doing those things that only please ourselves. One of two things is about to happen. The Word of the Lord, in Leviticus could take place and the judgment of God will be on our world as it was on Sodom and Gomorrah or the other option is that God, in His mercy, will raise up a generation of people like Phineas who will be zealous for righteousness. They will usher in a great world-wide revival, which would so permeate our society that sanity would be restored and Biblical rights and wrongs would be given their proper place. I am praying for a revival and a delaying of the judgment. But along with my prayers and those of millions of other believers there must also be a deliberate choice to repent, to live holy, and not allow evil to defile us.

Other books by Bartimaeus Publishing

To order any of these products contact:

REIGN MEDIA
777 Mokulele Hwy.
Kahului, HI 96732
Call Toll Free: 888-707-PRAY

Or Visit Us On The Web At:
www.kingscathedral.com
or
www.jamesmarocco.com